CURSIVE HANDWRITING WORKBOOK FOR KIDS

Jokes and Riddles

Welcome! EXL Cursive Handwriting Workbooks are designed to provide parents and teachers with **fun and motivational tools for helping students master cursive handwriting.**

Who Is This Workbook for?

Cursive Handwriting Workbook for Kids: Jokes and Riddles features 60 jokes for kids to trace and copy in cursive. Jokes make the practice fun, and therefore more effective! This workbook helps children practice writing full sentences in cursive **(Level 3)**. It is suitable for **grades 3 and up**.

Please have in mind that this workbook is not appropriate for beginners. It is addressed to students that have been taught to write the alphabet in cursive (Level 1) as well as words in cursive (Level 2).

How Is It Organized?

The exercises of this workbook are divided into two parts:

Part 1: Practice Pages

Trace and copy jokes in cursive. Students trace inside outlined words and then copy the sentences onto a new line. This part includes 60 practice pages.

Part 2: Advanced Practice

Rewrite printed sentences in cursive. All jokes are now in printed form and students have to rewrite them in cursive. This part includes 20 practice pages that will help children improve their cursive writing fluency.

At the back of this workbook, you will find **a handy cursive alphabet chart**.

Can I Photocopy This Workbook?

This workbook is reproducible! Feel free to photocopy parts of it to use at work or home!

- Parents who purchase a copy of this workbook may reproduce worksheets for their family members.
- Teachers who purchase a copy of this workbook may reproduce worksheets for their classes. However, teachers are not allowed to reproduce worksheets for other teachers or an entire school. Please encourage other teachers to buy their own copy!
- If you want to create worksheets with larger or smaller print, press the "enlarge/reduce" button on the copier's main menu and select the appropriate percentage.

If you have questions or ideas on how we can improve this workbook, please feel free to contact Victoria Vita at hellovictoriavita@gmail.com

Concept and layout design by Victoria Vita. Credits to Freepik for some of the graphics used.

The fonts used in producing this workbook can be purchased from Educational Fontware, Inc, www.educationalfontware.com. Special thanks to Mr. Dave Thompson of Educational Fontware, Inc for his kind support.

For questions, comments or ideas please contact: hellovictoriavita@gmail.com

ISBN-13: 978-1539762010

Part 1
Practice Pages
Trace and copy jokes in cursive

Tips!

- For a more pleasant and smoother writing experience **use a soft B pencil or rollerball pen** instead of a ballpoint pen. Choose one in your favorite color!

- Don't forget to **tilt the page!** If you are right-handed, tilt the page so that the lower left corner of the page is closer to you. If you are left-handed, tilt the page so that the lower right corner is closer to you. This paper position facilitates proper letter slant in your handwriting.

- When tracing inside the outlined words, try to be as accurate as you can. Tracing outlines – instead of just connecting dots – will help you **stay focused** on the exercise and refine your writing!

- When tracing or writing sentences, wait until all letters in a word are formed before going back to add any dots or crosses.

EXL **Name:**...
Cursive Handwriting Workbook for Kids: Jokes and Riddles

3

> *Why do cows wear bells?*
> *Because their*
> *horns don't work!*

Step 1: Practice by tracing inside the outlined letters with a pencil or pen!

Why do cows
wear bells?
Because their horns
don't work!

Step 2: Now copy the sentences in your best cursive writing!

_____
....
_____
_____
....
_____
_____
....
_____
_____

How well did you do?
Circle the face that shows how you feel about your progress!

Why didn't Cinderella make the basketball team? Because she ran away from the ball!

Step 1: Practice by tracing inside the outlined letters with a pencil or pen!

Why didn't Cinderella make the basketball team? Because she ran away from the ball!

Step 2: Now copy the sentences in your best cursive writing!

How well did you do?
Circle the face that shows how you feel about your progress!

What did the frog order at the dinner? French flies and a Diet Croak!

Step 1: Practice by tracing inside the outlined letters with a pencil or pen!

What did the frog order at the dinner? French flies and a Diet Croak!

Step 2: Now copy the sentences in your best cursive writing!

_____

....

_____

....

_____

_____

....

_____

_____

....

_____

How well did you do?
Circle the face that shows how you feel about your progress!

How does the ocean say hello?
It waves!

Step 1: Practice by tracing inside the outlined letters with a pencil or pen!

How does
the ocean say hello?
It waves!

Step 2: Now copy the sentences in your best cursive writing!

_____

. . . .

_____

_____

. . . .

_____

_____

. . . .

_____

_____

. . . .

_____

How well did you do?
Circle the face that shows how you feel about your progress!

Why did the scientist take out his doorbell? He wanted to win the no-bell prize!

Step 1: Practice by tracing inside the outlined letters with a pencil or pen!

Why did the scientist take out his doorbell? He wanted to win the no-bell prize!

Step 2: Now copy the sentences in your best cursive writing!

How well did you do?
Circle the face that shows how you feel about your progress!

Why couldn't the turkey eat dessert? Because he was stuffed!

Step 1: Practice by tracing inside the outlined letters with a pencil or pen!

Why couldn't the turkey eat dessert? Because he was stuffed!

Step 2: Now copy the sentences in your best cursive writing!

_____

....

_____

_____

....

_____

_____

....

_____

_____

....

_____

How well did you do?
Circle the face that shows how you feel about your progress!

What kind of flower do you never want to get on Valentine's Day? Cauliflower!

Step 1: Practice by tracing inside the outlined letters with a pencil or pen!

What kind of flower do you never want to get on Valentine's Day? Cauliflower!

Step 2: Now copy the sentences in your best cursive writing!

How well did you do?
Circle the face that shows how you feel about your progress!

What did zero say to eight?
Nice belt!

Step 1: Practice by tracing inside the outlined letters with a pencil or pen!

What did zero
say to eight?
Nice belt!

Step 2: Now copy the sentences in your best cursive writing!

How well did you do?
Circle the face that shows how you feel about your progress!

EXL **Name:**..
Cursive Handwriting Workbook for Kids: Jokes and Riddles

11

What kind of music are balloons afraid of? Pop Music!

Step 1: Practice by tracing inside the outlined letters with a pencil or pen!

What kind of music are balloons afraid of? Pop Music!

Step 2: Now copy the sentences in your best cursive writing!

How well did you do?
Circle the face that shows how you feel about your progress!

Name:...
Cursive Handwriting Workbook for Kids: Jokes and Riddles

12

Practice page 10

Why did Mickey Mouse
go to space?
He went to visit Pluto!

Step 1: Practice by tracing inside the outlined letters with a pencil or pen!

Why did
Mickey Mouse go to
space? He went to
visit Pluto!

Step 2: Now copy the sentences in your best cursive writing!

How well did you do?
Circle the face that shows how you feel about your progress!

Why can't you borrow money from an elf? Because they are always a little short!

Step 1: Practice by tracing inside the outlined letters with a pencil or pen!

Why can't you borrow money from an elf? Because they are always a little short!

Step 2: Now copy the sentences in your best cursive writing!

_____
....
_____
_____
....
_____
....
_____
_____
....
_____

How well did you do?
Circle the face that shows how you feel about your progress!

What is a photographer's
favorite food?
Cheese!

Step 1: Practice by tracing inside the outlined letters with a pencil or pen!

What is a
photographer's
favorite food?
Cheese!

Step 2: Now copy the sentences in your best cursive writing!

_____
....
_____
_____
....
_____
_____
....
_____

How well did you do?
Circle the face that shows how you feel about your progress!

What three candies do you find in school? Smarties, Dum-Dums and Nerds!

Step 1: Practice by tracing inside the outlined letters with a pencil or pen!

What three candies do you find in school? Smarties, Dum-Dums and Nerds!

Step 2: Now copy the sentences in your best cursive writing!

How well did you do?
Circle the face that shows how you feel about your progress!

What did elves learn in school?
The elf-abet!

Step 1: Practice by tracing inside the outlined letters with a pencil or pen!

What did elves
learn in school?
The elf-abet!

Step 2: Now copy the sentences in your best cursive writing!

How well did you do?
Circle the face that shows how you feel about your progress!

What keeps rock stars cool?
Their fans!

Step 1: Practice by tracing inside the outlined letters with a pencil or pen!

What keeps
rock stars cool?
Their fans!

Step 2: Now copy the sentences in your best cursive writing!

How well did you do?
Circle the face that shows how you feel about your progress!

EXL **Name:**
Cursive Handwriting Workbook for Kids: Jokes and Riddles

18

What is the biggest
kind of ant?
An eleph-ant!

Step 1: Practice by tracing inside the outlined letters with a pencil or pen!

What is the biggest
kind of ant?
An eleph-ant!

Step 2: Now copy the sentences in your best cursive writing!

How well did you do?
Circle the face that shows how you feel about your progress!

What is a monkey's favorite cookie? Chocolate Chimp!

Step 1: Practice by tracing inside the outlined letters with a pencil or pen!

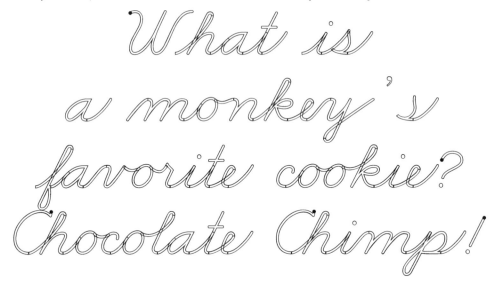

Step 2: Now copy the sentences in your best cursive writing!

How well did you do?
Circle the face that shows how you feel about your progress!

Name:..
Cursive Handwriting Workbook for Kids: Jokes and Riddles

20

What do you call a bear
with no teeth?
A gummy bear!

Step 1: Practice by tracing inside the outlined letters with a pencil or pen!

What do you
call a bear
with no teeth?
A gummy bear!

Step 2: Now copy the sentences in your best cursive writing!

How well did you do?
Circle the face that shows how you feel about your progress!

Where do you put barking dogs? In a barking lot!

Step 1: Practice by tracing inside the outlined letters with a pencil or pen!

Where do you put barking dogs? In a barking lot!

Step 2: Now copy the sentences in your best cursive writing!

How well did you do?
Circle the face that shows how you feel about your progress!

Why was the math book sad? It had too many problems!

Step 1: Practice by tracing inside outlined the letters with a pencil or pen!

Why was the math book sad? It had too many problems!

Step 2: Now copy the sentences in your best cursive writing!

How well did you do?
Circle the face that shows how you feel about your progress!

Why is six afraid of seven? Because seven eight nine!

Step 1: Practice by tracing inside the outlined letters with a pencil or pen!

Why is six afraid of seven? Because seven eight nine!

Step 2: Now copy the sentences in your best cursive writing!

How well did you do?
Circle the face that shows how you feel about your progress!

Name:...
EXL Cursive Handwriting Workbook for Kids: Jokes and Riddles

24

What do you get when you cross a pig and a dinosaur? Jurassic Pork!

Step 1: Practice by tracing inside the outlined letters with a pencil or pen!

What do you get when you cross a pig and a dinosaur? Jurassic Pork!

Step 2: Now copy the sentences in your best cursive writing!

How well did you do?
Circle the face that shows how you feel about your progress!

How did the barber
win the race?
He knew a short cut!

Step 1: Practice by tracing inside the outlined letters with a pencil or pen!

How did the barber
win the race?
He knew
a short cut!

Step 2: Now copy the sentences in your best cursive writing!

How well did you do?
Circle the face that shows how you feel about your progress!

Why was Peter sitting
on his watch?
He wanted to be on time!

Step 1: Practice by tracing inside the outlined letters with a pencil or pen!

Why was Peter
sitting on his
watch? He wanted
to be on time!

Step 2: Now copy the sentences in your best cursive writing!

How well did you do?
Circle the face that shows how you feel about your progress!

EXL **Name:**

Cursive Handwriting Workbook for Kids: Jokes and Riddles

What dog can jump higher than a house? Any dog - a house can't jump!

Step 1: Practice by tracing inside the outlined letters with a pencil or pen!

What dog can jump higher than a house? Any dog - a house can't jump!

Step 2: Now copy the sentences in your best cursive writing!

How well did you do?
Circle the face that shows how you feel about your progress!

What kind of music
do mummies like?
Wrap music!

Step 1: Practice by tracing inside the outlined letters with a pencil or pen!

What kind of music
do mummies like?
Wrap music!

Step 2: Now copy the sentences in your best cursive writing!

How well did you do?
Circle the face that shows how you feel about your progress!

Practice page 27

Why can't a bicycle stand up? Because it is two-tired (too tired)!

Step 1: Practice by tracing inside the outlined letters with a pencil or pen!

Why can't a bicycle stand up? Because it is two-tired (too tired)!

Step 2: Now copy the sentences in your best cursive writing!

How well did you do?
Circle the face that shows how you feel about your progress!

Name:

EXL Cursive Handwriting Workbook for Kids: Jokes and Riddles

30

What kind of bee
can't make up its mind?
A maybe!

Step 1: Practice by tracing inside the outlined letters with a pencil or pen!

What kind of bee
can't make up
its mind?
A maybe!

Step 2: Now copy the sentences in your best cursive writing!

How well did you do?
Circle the face that shows how you feel about your progress!

In what school do you learn how to greet people? In Hi School!

Step 1: Practice by tracing inside the outlined letters with a pencil or pen!

In what school do you learn how to greet people? In Hi School!

Step 2: Now copy the sentences in your best cursive writing!

How well did you do?
Circle the face that shows how you feel about your progress!

Name:...

What's the best place
to grow flowers in school?
In kindergarden!

Step 1: Practice by tracing inside the outlined letters with a pencil or pen!

What's the best place
to grow flowers
in school?
In kindergarden!

Step 2: Now copy the sentences in your best cursive writing!

_____

....

_____

....

_____

....

_____

....

_____

....

How well did you do?
Circle the face that shows how you feel about your progress!

What school subject is a witch good at? Spelling!

Step 1: Practice by tracing inside the outlined letters with a pencil or pen!

What school subject is a witch good at? Spelling!

Step 2: Now copy the sentences in your best cursive writing!

_____

_____

_____

_____

_____

_____

How well did you do?
Circle the face that shows how you feel about your progress!

What do you call
a flying policeman?
A helicopper!

Step 1: Practice by tracing inside the outlined letters with a pencil or pen!

What do you call
a flying policeman?
A helicopper!

Step 2: Now copy the sentences in your best cursive writing!

How well did you do?
Circle the face that shows how you feel about your progress!

Why is Peter Pan always flying? Because he can never neverland!

Step 1: Practice by tracing inside the outlined letters with a pencil or pen!

Why is Peter Pan
always flying?
Because he can
never neverland!

Step 2: Now copy the sentences in your best cursive writing!

How well did you do?
Circle the face that shows how you feel about your progress!

Which alphabet letter helps you duplicate yourself? The W(Double You)!

Step 1: Practice by tracing inside the outlined letters with a pencil or pen!

Which alphabet letter helps you duplicate yourself? The W (Double You)!

Step 2: Now copy the sentences in your best cursive writing!

How well did you do?
Circle the face that shows how you feel about your progress!

Practice page 35

Why can't dogs use the DVD remote? They can only hit the paws (pause) button!

Step 1: Practice by tracing inside the outlined letters with a pencil or pen!

Why can't dogs use
the DVD remote?
They can only hit the
paws (pause) button!

Step 2: Now copy the sentences in your best cursive writing!

How well did you do?
Circle the face that shows how you feel about your progress!

Name:

Cursive Handwriting Workbook for Kids: Jokes and Riddles

38

What did one elevator say to the other? I think I am coming down with something!

Step 1: Practice by tracing inside the letters with a pencil or pen!

What did one elevator

say to the other?

I think I am coming

down with something!

Step 2: Now copy the sentences in your best cursive writing!

_____

_____

_____

_____

_____

_____

_____

How well did you do?
Circle the face that shows how you feel about your progress!

What kind of dog can tell the time? A watch dog!

Step 1: Practice by tracing inside the outlined letters with a pencil or pen!

What kind of dog can tell the time? A watch dog!

Step 2: Now copy the sentences in your best cursive writing!

How well did you do?
Circle the face that shows how you feel about your progress!

Which fruit absolutely loves cocoa? A coconut!

Step 1: Practice by tracing inside the outlined letters with a pencil or pen!

Which fruit absolutely loves cocoa? A coconut!

Step 2: Now copy the sentences in your best cursive writing!

How well did you do?
Circle the face that shows how you feel about your progress!

What kind of fish is famous?
A star-fish!

Step 1: Practice by tracing inside the outlined letters with a pencil or pen!

What kind of
fish is famous?
A star-fish!

Step 2: Now copy the sentences in your best cursive writing!

How well did you do?
Circle the face that shows how you feel about your progress!

What do you call cheese
that is not your cheese?
Nacho Cheese!

Step 1: Practice by tracing inside the outlined letters with a pencil or pen!

What do you call
cheese that is
not your cheese?
Nacho Cheese!

Step 2: Now copy the sentences in your best cursive writing!

How well did you do?
Circle the face that shows how you feel about your progress!

What do you get if you pamper a cow? Spoiled milk!

Step 1: Practice by tracing inside the outlined letters with a pencil or pen!

What do you get if you pamper a cow? Spoiled milk!

Step 2: Now copy the sentences in your best cursive writing!

How well did you do?
Circle the face that shows how you feel about your progress!

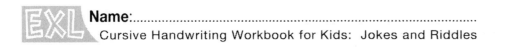

Where do bees
go to the bathroom?
The BP station!

Step 1: Practice by tracing inside the outlined letters with a pencil or pen!

Where do bees
go to the bathroom?
The BP station!

Step 2: Now copy the sentences in your best cursive writing!

_____
....
_____
....
_____
....
_____
....
_____
....

How well did you do?
Circle the face that shows how you feel about your progress!

EXL **Name:**..

Cursive Handwriting Workbook for Kids: Jokes and Riddles

What season is it when you go on a trampoline? Springtime!

Step 1: Practice by tracing inside the outlined letters with a pencil or pen!

What season is it when you go on a trampoline? Springtime!

Step 2: Now copy the sentences in your best cursive writing!

How well did you do?
Circle the face that shows how you feel about your progress!

What is a tornado's
favorite game to play?
Twister!

Step 1: Practice by tracing inside the outlined letters with a pencil or pen!

What is
a tornado's favorite
game to play?
Twister!

Step 2: Now copy the sentences in your best cursive writing!

_____

....

_____

_____

....

_____

_____

....

_____

_____

....

_____

How well did you do?
Circle the face that shows how you feel about your progress!

Name:...

Cursive Handwriting Workbook for Kids: Jokes and Riddles

What kind of tree
can fit into your hand?
A palm tree!

Step 1: Practice by tracing inside the outlined letters with a pencil or pen!

What kind of tree
can fit
into your hand?
A palm tree!

Step 2: Now copy the sentences in your best cursive writing!

How well did you do?
Circle the face that shows how you feel about your progress!

Name:

Why was the little ant so confused? Because all his uncles were "ants"!

Step 1: Practice by tracing inside the outlined letters with a pencil or pen!

Why was the little ant so confused? Because all his uncles were "ants"!

Step 2: Now copy the sentences in your best cursive writing!

_____
....
_____
....
_____
_____
....
_____
_____
....
_____

How well did you do?
Circle the face that shows how you feel about your progress!

Name:...
Cursive Handwriting Workbook for Kids: Jokes and Riddles

49

What does a skeleton say before he eats? BONE appetite!

Step 1: Practice by tracing inside the outlined letters with a pencil or pen!

What does a skeleton say before he eats? BONE appetite!

Step 2: Now copy the sentences in your best cursive writing!

How well did you do?
Circle the face that shows how you feel about your progress!

Who always comes to a picnic
but is never invited?
Ants!

Step 1: Practice by tracing inside the outlined letters with a pencil or pen!

Who always
comes to a picnic
but is never invited?
Ants!

Step 2: Now copy the sentences in your best cursive writing!

_____
....
_____
....
_____
....
_____
....
_____

How well did you do?
Circle the face that shows how you feel about your progress!

Name:...

EXL   Cursive Handwriting Workbook for Kids: Jokes and Riddles

Why were the Middle Ages called the Dark Ages? Because there were so many knights!

Step 1: Practice by tracing inside the outlined letters with a pencil or pen!

Why were the Middle Ages called the Dark Ages? Because there were so many knights!

Step 2: Now copy the sentences in your best cursive writing!

_____

_____

_____

_____

_____

_____

How well did you do?
Circle the face that shows how you feel about your progress!

Name:...
Cursive Handwriting Workbook for Kids: Jokes and Riddles

52

What do you give
to a sick lemon?
Lemon aid!

Step 1: Practice by tracing inside the outlined letters with a pencil or pen!

What do you give
to a sick lemon?
Lemon aid!

Step 2: Now copy the sentences in your best cursive writing!

How well did you do?
Circle the face that shows how you feel about your progress!

What is a cheetah's favorite food? Fast food!

Step 1: Practice by tracing inside the outlined letters with a pencil or pen!

What is a cheetah's favorite food? Fast food!

Step 2: Now copy the sentences in your best cursive writing!

How well did you do?
Circle the face that shows how you feel about your progress!

Why are fish so smart?
Because they are always
in a school!

Step 1: Practice by tracing inside the outlined letters with a pencil or pen!

Why are fish
so smart?
Because they are
always in a school!

Step 2: Now copy the sentences in your best cursive writing!

How well did you do?
Circle the face that shows how you feel about your progress!

Why can't the elephant use the computer? Because he is afraid of the mouse!

Step 1: Practice by tracing inside the outlined letters with a pencil or pen!

Why can't the elephant use the computer? Because he is afraid of the mouse!

Step 2: Now copy the sentences in your best cursive writing!

How well did you do?
Circle the face that shows how you feel about your progress!

EXL **Name:**..
Cursive Handwriting Workbook for Kids: Jokes and Riddles

Why do cowboys ride horses?
Because they are too heavy
to carry!

Step 1: Practice by tracing inside the outlined letters with a pencil or pen!

Why do cowboys
ride horses?
Because they are
too heavy to carry!

Step 2: Now copy the sentences in your best cursive writing!

How well did you do?
Circle the face that shows how you feel about your progress!

Name:

Cursive Handwriting Workbook for Kids: Jokes and Riddles

Why didn't the oven go to college? Because it had a lot of degrees already!

Step 1: Practice by tracing inside the outlined letters with a pencil or pen!

Why didn't the oven go to college? Because it had a lot of degrees already!

Step 2: Now copy the sentences in your best cursive writing!

How well did you do?
Circle the face that shows how you feel about your progress!

EXL **Name:**
Cursive Handwriting Workbook for Kids: Jokes and Riddles

Where do cows go on Friday night? They go to the Mooovie theater!

Step 1: Practice by tracing inside the outlined letters with a pencil or pen!

Where do cows go on Friday night? They go to the Mooovie theater!

Step 2: Now copy the sentences in your best cursive writing!

_____

....

_____

....

_____

....

_____

....

_____

How well did you do?
Circle the face that shows how you feel about your progress!

Name:..
Cursive Handwriting Workbook for Kids: Jokes and Riddles

What is a cat's favorite color? Purr-ple!

Step 1: Practice by tracing inside the outlined letters with a pencil or pen!

What is a cat's favorite color? Purr-ple!

Step 2: Now copy the sentences in your best cursive writing!

How well did you do?
Circle the face that shows how you feel about your progress!

Why did the banana go to the doctor? It wasn't peeling well!

Step 1: Practice by tracing inside the outlined letters with a pencil or pen!

Why did the banana go to the doctor? It wasn't peeling well!

Step 2: Now copy the sentences in your best cursive writing!

How well did you do?
Circle the face that shows how you feel about your progress!

Name:...

Cursive Handwriting Workbook for Kids: Jokes and Riddles

What do you get when you cross a caterpillar and a talking parrot? A walky talkie!

Step 1: Practice by tracing inside the outlined letters with a pencil or pen!

What do you get when you cross a caterpillar and a talking parrot? A walky talkie!

Step 2: Now copy the sentences in your best cursive writing!

How well did you do?
Circle the face that shows how you feel about your progress!

Name:..
Cursive Handwriting Workbook for Kids: Jokes and Riddles

What do you call an owl
that does magic tricks?
Hooooo -dini!

Step 1: Practice by tracing inside the outlined letters with a pencil or pen!

What do you call
an owl that
does magic tricks?
Hooooo -dini!

Step 2: Now copy the sentences in your best cursive writing!

How well did you do?
Circle the face that shows how you feel about your progress!

Part 2
Advanced Practice
Rewrite printed sentences in cursive

Tips!

- If you are not sure how to form a letter, check the cursive alphabet chart at the back of this book.
- The following uppercase letters **do not connect** to lowercase letters in a word: **B, D, F, G, I, L, O, P, Q, S, T, V, W**
- The following uppercase letters connect to lowercase letters in a word: **A, C, E, H, J, K, M, N, R, U, X, Y, Z**
- When writing sentences, wait until all letters in a word are formed before going back to add any dots or crosses.

Why do cows wear bells?
Because their horns don't work!

_____

. . . .

_____

_____

. . . .

_____

Why didn't Cinderella make the basketball team?
Because she ran away from the ball!

_____

. . . .

_____

_____

. . . .

_____

How does the ocean say hello?
It waves!

_____

. . . .

_____

_____

. . . .

_____

What did the frog order at the dinner?
French flies and a Diet Croak!

_____
....
_____
....
_____
....
_____

Why did the scientist take out his doorbell?
He wanted to win the no-bell prize!

_____
....
_____
....
_____
....
_____

Why couldn't the turkey eat dessert?
Because he was stuffed!

_____
....
_____
....
_____
....
_____

EXL **Name:**..
Cursive Handwriting Workbook for Kids: Jokes and Riddles

66

What kind of flower do you never want to get on Valentine's Day?
Cauliflower!

What did zero say to eight?
Nice belt!

What kind of music are balloons afraid of?
Pop Music!

Name: ....
Cursive Handwriting Workbook for Kids: Jokes and Riddles

67

Why did Mickey Mouse go to space?
He went to visit Pluto!

Why can't you borrow money from an elf?
Because they are always a little short!

What is a photographer's favorite food?
Cheese!

EXL **Name:**..
Cursive Handwriting Workbook for Kids: Jokes and Riddles

68

What three candies do you find in school?
Smarties, Dum-Dums and Nerds!

What did elves learn in school?
The elf-abet!

What keeps rock stars cool?
Their fans!

What is the biggest kind of ant?
An eleph-ant!

_____

. . . .

_____

_____

. . . .

_____

_____

. . . .

_____

What is a monkey's favorite cookie?
Chocolate Chimp!

_____

. . . .

_____

_____

. . . .

_____

_____

. . . .

_____

What do you call a bear with no teeth?
A gummy bear!

_____

. . . .

_____

_____

. . . .

_____

_____

. . . .

_____

EXL **Name:** . . . .

Cursive Handwriting Workbook for Kids: Jokes and Riddles

70

Where do you put barking dogs?
In a barking lot!

_____
....
_____
_____
....
_____
_____
....
_____

Why was the math book sad?
It had too many problems!

_____
....
_____
_____
....
_____
_____
....
_____

Why is six afraid of seven?
Because seven eight nine!

_____
....
_____
_____
....
_____
_____
....
_____

What do you get when you cross a pig and a dinosaur?
Jurassic Pork!

_____

. . . .

_____

_____

. . . .

_____

_____

How did the barber win the race?
He knew a short cut!

_____

. . . .

_____

_____

. . . .

_____

_____

. . . .

_____

Why was Peter sitting on his watch?
He wanted to be on time!

_____

. . . .

_____

_____

. . . .

_____

_____

. . . .

_____

What dog can jump higher than a house?
Any dog – a house can't jump!

_____
. . . .
_____
_____
. . . .
_____

What kind of music do mummies like?
Wrap music!

_____
. . . .
_____
_____
. . . .
_____

Why can't a bicycle stand up?
Because it is two-tired (too tired)!

_____
. . . .
_____
_____
. . . .
_____

What kind of bee can't make up its mind?
A maybe!

In what school do you learn how to greet people?
In Hi School!

What's the best place to grow flowers in school?
In kindergarden!

Name:...
Cursive Handwriting Workbook for Kids: Jokes and Riddles

74

What school subject is a witch good at?
Spelling!

_____

. . . .

_____

_____

. . . .

_____

_____

. . . .

_____

What do you call a flying policeman?
A helicopper!

_____

. . . .

_____

_____

. . . .

_____

_____

. . . .

_____

Why is Peter Pan always flying?
Because he can never neverland!

_____

. . . .

_____

_____

. . . .

_____

_____

. . . .

_____

What alphabet letter helps you duplicate yourself?
The W (Double You)!

_____

_____

_____

_____

_____

Why can't dogs use the DVD remote?
Because they can only hit the paws (pause) button!

_____

_____

_____

_____

_____

What did one elevator say to the other?
I think I am coming down with something!

_____

_____

_____

_____

_____

What kind of dog can tell the time?
A watch dog!

_____

Which fruit absolutely loves cocoa?
A coconut!

_____

What kind of fish is famous?
A star-fish!

_____

Name:...
Cursive Handwriting Workbook for Kids: Jokes and Riddles

77

What do you call cheese that is not your cheese?
Nacho Cheese!

_____
....
_____
....
_____
....
_____

What do you get if you pamper a cow?
Spoiled milk!

_____
....
_____
....
_____
....
_____

Where do bees go to the bathroom?
The BP station!

_____
....
_____
....
_____
....
_____

What season is it when you go on a trampoline?
Springtime!

What is a tornado's favorite game to play?
Twister!

What kind of tree can fit into your hand?
A palm tree!

Why was the little ant so confused?
Because all his uncles were "ants"!

_____

....

_____

....

_____

....

_____

What does a skeleton say before he eats?
BONE appetite!

_____

....

_____

....

_____

....

_____

Who always comes to a picnic but is never invited?
Ants!

_____

....

_____

....

_____

....

_____

EXL **Name:**..
Cursive Handwriting Workbook for Kids: Jokes and Riddles

80

Why were the Middle Ages called the Dark Ages?
Because there were so many knights!

_____

....

_____

_____

....

_____

What do you give to a sick lemon?
Lemon aid!

_____

....

_____

_____

....

_____

What is a cheetah's favorite food?
Fast food!

_____

....

_____

_____

....

_____

Name:...
Cursive Handwriting Workbook for Kids: Jokes and Riddles

81

Why are fish so smart?
Because they are always in a school!

_____
....
_____
....
_____
....
_____
....
_____

Why can't the elephant use the computer?
Because he is afraid of the mouse!

_____
....
_____
....
_____
....
_____
....
_____

Why do cowboys ride horses?
Because they are too heavy to carry!

_____
....
_____
....
_____
....
_____
....
_____

EXL **Name:**..
Cursive Handwriting Workbook for Kids: Jokes and Riddles

82

Why didn't the oven go to college?
It had a lot of degrees already!

_____

. . . .

_____

_____

_____

_____

_____

. . . .

_____

Where do cows go on Friday night?
They go to the Mooovie theater!

_____

. . . .

_____

. . . .

_____

_____

. . . .

_____

What is a cat's favorite color?
Purr-ple!

_____

. . . .

_____

. . . .

_____

. . . .

_____

Why did the banana go to the doctor?
It wasn't peeling well!

_____

....

_____

_____

....

_____

_____

....

_____

What do you get when you cross a caterpillar and a talking parrot?
A walky talkie!

_____

....

_____

_____

....

_____

_____

....

_____

What do you call an owl that knows magic?
Hooooo-dini!

_____

....

_____

_____

....

_____

_____

....

_____

Cursive alphabet chart

Uppercase and lowercase cursive letters

$A\ a$

$B\ b$

$C\ c$

$D\ d$

$E\ e$

$F\ f$

$G\ g$

$H\ h$

$I\ i$

$J\ j$

$K\ k$

$L\ l$

$M\ m$

$N\ n$

O o

P p

Q q

R r

S s

T t

U u

V v

W w

X x

Y y

Z z

0 1 2 3 4 5 6 7 8 9

These uppercase letters **do not** connect to lowercase letters: **B, D, F, G, I, L, O, P, Q, S, T, V, W**
These uppercase letters connect to lowercase letters: **A, C, E, H, J, K, M, N, R, U, X, Y, Z**

Hi!

My name is Victoria Vita.
My team I worked hard to create this workbook!
If you enjoyed it and found it useful,
please ask your mom or dad to help you
write a review on Amazon!
Your kind reviews and honest comments
will encourage us
to keep making more books like this!
Thank you!

Victoria Vita

Ps. If you have comments or ideas on how we can improve
this workbook, feel free to contact me
at my personal email:
hellovictoriavita@gmail.com

Made in the USA
San Bernardino, CA
21 May 2019